THE BATTLE AGAINST
MENTAL ILLNESS

FACT OR FANTASY TO BE KEPT UNSTABLE AND CRAZY

THE BATTLE AGAINST MENTAL ILLNESS

The Chapters in My Life

KELSEY FOOTE

Library of Congress Control Number: 2023913741
ISBN: Hardcover   979-8-3694-0373-0
             Softcover   979-8-3694-0372-3
             eBook   979-8-3694-0371-6

Print information available on the last page.

Rev. date: 07/31/2023

To order additional copies of this book, contact:
Xlibris
844-714-8691
www.Xlibris.com
Orders@Xlibris.com
848914

I was very blessed and fortunate, not to mention sheltered, in my childhood. I grew up in a small community surrounded by love with parents, grandparents, and great-grandparents— not to mention a community of aunts, uncles, cousins, and friends who had my back, and their intent was usually good. Growing up I was very active and had no interest in men. I focused on myself and was always blessed by meeting many nice young men and true gentlemen by all accounts. I realize I was fortunate and blessed when I look back. God, my angels, and my prayer warriors were there through all this as my life took unexpected turns.

Unfortunately, like so many, not all has been good, and despite all the lows that came into my life, I managed to believe in and still expect the best of others. What is the saying that goes something like "the heart wants what the heart wants"? My choice may not have been the best, and so many options I passed up might have been better, but I believe that is why it is called life. Life is never easy, and there is no utopia. And although there were good times, there were lows too, like a roller coaster.

I believe I am a fighter and a warrior or else I would not be here. And faith tells us that God never gives us more than we can handle. I look back at times and wonder how I survived and got to this point. There are so many stories out there, and we need to focus on the positive.

I was and have been blessed in so many ways—the real focus here is on mental illness. Illness is not something to be taken lightly, but sometimes it is best to be left in the dark because the stigma it puts on a person might not be a good thing. Not to mention if the medical professional or a loved one tainted you and others' perceptions of you. Sadly, *he* was the believed one and the one with the voice; I was the ill one with the mental illness and had no voice. We are all humans and make mistakes, but we are not just numbers, nor should we be tarnished by the powerful ones with a voice. Who is the patient? Who should be heard? I look back and know I was made to be the sick one by a man who controlled me, dominated me, and played the good old man while bad-mouthing me to all and anyone who would listen—his manipulative ways and traits, his world, and I was the stranger. And so started my world of mental illness. I, like so many others, was misdiagnosed, and many played a role in this direction of my life. How could I let this happen to me? I did. I always thought I was the strong, independent woman who survived. But in this marriage, I took my vows to heart and believed them. I don't say this lightly, but I never cheated. I always stood by him despite all his shit and grief, which was of course always my fault—which led to my demise and broken spirit or being his shadow. Between him and the professional doctors, my spirit was broken. How I came back and regained my fight, passion, and sense of humor I will never know. I would say faith and my passions and my will to survive and fight. Also a good family who stood by me. Between him (his mother and family) and the doctors, their main goal was to drug me, and they laughed at me when I told them I never did drugs—pot, no; hard drugs, not once. My first alcoholic drink was at the age of twenty-one, and my sexual encounters are two. I passed a lie detector when we first were married and offered a job with the FBI. How could I have let this happen to me? Could that be why I was deemed the crazy mental one with issues? My hell started, and the roller coaster ride began.

God, there must be a reason for my journey or the road you had me take. Imagine having a sick, evil stalker rob and torment you for years and then your friends tell you there is no reason to get upset over a few missing items now and then. Do you know what it does to an individual to come home and find missing items, many with sentimental value? There is a feeling of never being safe again, especially in your home. There is torment and feelings of helplessness when there's a sick, evil creep coming into your home—*your home*. Finding a gift of a stool sample in your toilet and grease on your carpet and your bed all messed up, and then having an upstanding police sergeant tell you that you are lonely and it's your stool sample and that you are looking for attention. I am lucky they didn't press charges against me for making up such bizarre stories. What an imagination I have.

Do you know what living in fear for your life is like? How is that good for you? The universe puts you in situations like this, so there must be a reason for it. I do not believe so, and this fighting is not God's will. This is a sicko individual, and I have no damn clue who this jerk is, and I continue to be at his lousy mercy. I thank God, and my faith keeps me going. I may be crazy, but I refuse to run—I prefer to stand my ground. Nobody deserves this—nobody. And where is the good neighbor? Do you know how this feels? I pray you never do. If you have had one theft, think of that feeling. Then to have it done and done again there's a helpless feeling, violation at the mercy of a sicko. How does one deal with that? And I am the crazy one. All in my head. How do I even leave my home? To this day I will never know. Also, you should see the lists I have of missing items. And people tell me not to get concerned over a few. What a sick joke. And what the hell is a security system for? What a joke—paying for a service that does not work.

Can you think of the damage this does to a person? To the mind, to trust? And in your own home—what a sick, evil loser this creep is. I am the sick one with the mental illness. If I was so sick and not of sound judgement, how could I have dealt with this all this time? Could you? I ask you again: could you? I have no clue. My prayer is that he has the courage to come when I am home. What does this tell you about this sicko? I have lost my voice again in this matter. I still have no voice and a joke of a security system. This is the same feeling I had with my beloved husband. And how did he protect me? Yet here I am fighting an unknown assailant. When you lose your voice and are being controlled, it's easy for this to happen. Laugh all you want—I let it happen in my marriage as well, but it happened. Why would someone you love so much do this to you?

When things were good, *wow*. He was all mine, a gentleman, and he gave me his attention. I think to him I was the chase and challenge. I had avoided so many men, and he had women fawning over him. I was a challenge. Once he won me, it was over—with the ring on my finger I became a doormat. He knew my loyalty and love. He could trust me all he wanted with nothing to worry about while he did whatever he wanted. And I would be there. The only issue was I had a voice and strength and would stand up for myself in the beginning—but that would not last.

I would ask a veteran how he or she felt after having to fight for his or her life and country. How he or she felt and if that feeling has ever left him or her. Can veterans talk about it? I remember my father telling me that on a hunting trip with his male friends they had met some women, and he went back to the room. That's what I wanted. Mine was a love of torment. He knew he had me and the type of woman I was, so he verbally abused me, used me, and walked on me. I was a doormat, his slave, mother, housekeeper, and the woman who stood behind him through all his betrayals. I was still there standing by his side and giving him support through all his destructive behavior. Yet I was the crazy one? Thankfully, physical abuse was not him, and he could be a good man who would go all heights for anyone but me, or so it seemed. I could not persuade him, but his family and mentors sure could. Yet everything that happened in our life was my fault even though I was not the one making the choices or decisions. I learned to apologize and take the blame. Half the time I didn't even know what I had done. Why did I smile at him? Why did I say that? Did I laugh? Did I cry?

My story is of mental illness, and I believe it needs to be heard, taken seriously—let the patient be the voice. How can a woman who went from postpartum depression to split personality, to bipolar and suicidal—and, of course, I learned, child abuse—get up every morning out of her bed and have laughter, have will, have fight? How? I ask this: why did the doctors listen to my husband and his voice? Where was my voice? I was supposed to be the ill one—the patient—I went to one appointment alone and never was able to go back to that doctor because he advised me, that I was misdiagnosed and over-drugged. First and last appointment alone, when my family and friends asked my family what was wrong with me . I was clearly overmedicated,, yet my husband went along with this, and the doctors prescribed and listened to the good old boy because of his family and their status.

Where was my voice? My main intent now is to be heard, and I want anyone who is going through or has gone through this to be heard. I want doctors to hear this as well. I know they are the educated ones and the professionals, but sometimes not all is as it is made out to be.

At the age of twenty-four—it's all in the timing, I hear—I gave my heart, and there was no looking back. The man who won my heart was not at all what my family and friends expected. Again, I guess it goes to what the heart wants, the timing, vulnerability, and the fact that he was smart. My courtship was fast and furious; he courted me, wined and dined me, took me dancing, out to dinner, and skiing. He was attentive, romantic, filled with laughter and was there for me! I didn't see the signs or changes that would come. I was swept off my feet and played by a charmer when he wanted me to be. I was naïve and excited that I had found someone I wanted to grow old with and hold hands with, the person to share my life, with the white picket fence, children, dreams, and goals.

How could something so good take such wrong turns—unhappy homelife, bitterness, weakness in his love of women, and need to be the center of attention. He had me, but no one else would; he made sure of that. I really had my eyes closed and was so excited at our future, but I had no clue of what I was getting into or the control his mother had over him or how easily he could be influenced by others even as I had no voice with him. Life with him was all his way or the highway, and I let it be that way. I allowed it. We were both passionate and strong willed, and fights definitely happened until I became the mental patient—passive—and his dominant control began. *Be the good girl and do exactly what he says.* Yet he would be telling others different stories.

I am not normal in today's world. I gave him my entire heart and went all in. This was a life commitment to my future life as a family. This was not changing socks or beds. I took my vow seriously—again, maybe that's why I was the sick, mental one. I do not fit into any category, and I believe there should be no categories. We are who we are and most doing the best we can. My first full-fledged sexual encounter was my college boyfriend, and I was in love with him. I thought we would have a future. He graduated a year earlier than I did and being who I was, my first priority was to finish my college, especially because I only had one year to go. Distance makes the heart grow fonder or tend to wander? He went back home and ended up getting someone pregnant and marrying her. When I met my husband, it was definitely not a rebound, and more than three years of dating showed me we had a lasting love.

Love has not always come easily for me, and I don't give my heart easily (I think I envy those who can). There were some men I met whom I wish I could have loved, but that was not in the cards. I am told I close the door too quickly, but I would rather end something than end up hurting someone. I would not want that to happen to me, and I would not want to do it to someone else. In my marriage, it was only my husband. Of course, I would look and maybe a couple times be tempted when a man approached me and my husband was off doing his thing with no clue I was being approached. Of course, I felt like the man had to be an idiot to be interested in me. I believed I was ugly and worthless and my poor husband had to put up with me and all my faults and failings.

I also know I did not have his mother's approval; I didn't realize how much his control his mother had: -his mother came before me in all areas. A mother should be important in a man's life, but when he takes on a wife, she should come first. He should have had room for both of us. I look back and realize I always came last and really didn't count. In the beginning, I believe I did have his mother's approval and was the one you take home to your mother or the girl next door. When he married me, I expected to come first with our family—his family—but sadly, if his mother called he jumped, and if I needed something I would always come last.

It is not a good feeling and doesn't do a lot for a person's ego when he or she always comes last, has no voice, and never seems to do anything right. I could throw a dinner party for twenty or more people, bake, cook, do all the laundry, ironing, cleaning inside and a lot of times outside the house. I didn't mind; I loved being a wife and mother and all that came along. I knew marriage was work and not easy. I believe in compromise, not always agreeing but being able to have a voice. Spouses should be best friends and have each other's back and be safe with each other. They should protect and support each other and work together. Maybe I watched too many Hallmark movies or read too many romance novels. Life always throws curves, and there are good and bad times and you work through all of them together. You don't run or betray each other. Sadly, I should have stuck to romance books and the Hallmark channel.

As they say, mothers know best My mother is a bit of a psychic, and she advised me not to rush in to our romance. It was a six-month romance and engagement as well as long distance, but I was so madly in love and happy at the time I saw no warning signs, only bliss. A whirlwind romance can work, but sadly, mine did not work the way I wanted or had hoped.

Our courtship was fast and furious, and I think my holding off on not jumping into his bed was a thrill to him and one that he was not used too. I think women had been easy conquests for him, so I guess I fit the image of the good girl and the one to take home to his mother. I look back and think he didn't respect me because I stood behind what I said. He was more *do what I say*, and his behavior definitely did not support that talk. Please, women, don't take offense; I was told if I was bought dinner that I was expected to spend the night in that's man's bed, but that's not me. Maybe my life would have been easier if I had more of that mentality, and yet I am not a nun. For me to get in bed with a man, I have to have my heart there. I am as passionate as anyone and not a prude. In my widowed years, I told someone that I would buy my own damn dinner.

My husband gave me the butterflies—there was definitely chemistry there. It took three to four months for our first lovemaking and our engagement to happen, and we were married a year later.

Things happened quickly in our life together and for me: I packed up, quit my job, and moved into his home. I gave up everything for love, including myself in the end as it happened. I should have seen the warning signs but was deeply in love and excited at the thought of marriage and spending my life with him. Only the dynamics of his family or how tight-knit they were and his mother the matriarch would rule our world. I went from confident to being treated as if I were wrong all the time and apologizing constantly when I did not even know what I had done wrong. I was the bad guy, and he was the poor man who had to put up with me, the crazy mental woman—his wife. Poor, poor hubby.

My life was never my own again, and when I didn't play by their rules, I always suffered a consequence and usually not a happy one We were both passionate and stubborn. Verbal fights were normal in our marriage, and when I gave up and became silent there was peace. Or he and the doctor had me so over prescribed I would just sleep or go along. His family are not nice people but were big in the church. I do not judge, yet do we go to church to thank God for all we are blessed with, or is hell and damnation for all our sins we committed or didn't. I am not against church or the feeling you get when you visit one. I went to church every Sunday for many years. The community I have not always understood—were they looking out for one another, or it was a matter of keeping one's enemies close? I am a believer, and each to his or her own, whatever works best. I also fought fair and played by the rules. I went from being independent to being dependent and my husband's shadow. I lost myself totally: No voice! No me!

After I had my son, I cried easily, and I was definitely a type A personality— house clean, clothes washed, and dinner on the table. I was blessed as a cook thanks to my mom and her chef abilities in the kitchen. I remember our first fight in marriage occurred because I made chili with pinto beans, not kidney beans. I did not know what pinto beans were (I knew of kidney beans). Of course, it didn't meet my husband's expectations, but his friend thought it was delicious. Such a small fight to lose sleep over. No battle was small. Everything and anything I did was wrong and turned into a battle to my husband, and I never seemed to do anything right. My husband didn't know how to pick battles or compromise: it was his way or the highway. The biggest and one battle I won was over life insurance, and it involved the whole insurance team; they still remember it to this day, twenty-some years later. I was "greedy and a gold digger." I only wanted to protect our family, and his family did not believe in insurance. We ended up with life insurance, and not a million dollars as family rumors had it, but that's nice thought. More power to them in destroying me or what was left of me.

I really don't see myself as that attractive or desirable. I look back and I think what started my husband's and family's belief that I was a traitor. I met a man while I was engaged, and a what a true gentleman he was. I was upfront with him, and he said you have not walked down the aisle yet—no marriage and no wedding ring yet. What a gentleman and a man woman desired and to know they existed. Wow, and he was interested in me. We didn't have cell phones at that time. I gave him my in-laws' family number because he wanted to talk to me before I walked down the aisle. He called me at my in-laws' house, and I was advised there was a man on the phone. All he asked is if he still had a chance or I was going to go through with the wedding. I said the wedding was on and never heard from him again. When I got off the phone, the whole environment was a frigid zone. I asked my then-fiancé if we could talk in private, and he said no! He already knew what was going on. I tried again on the way home, and he didn't give me chance. He told me not to waste his time.

Sadly, I never knew their side of the story was that I was cheating on him up to our wedding day, and I thought I was being upfront. If I had had anything to hide, I would not have had him call me at my in–laws'. I should have seen the communication dangers there. I was so stupid—the rumors were flying from that night on about cheating, being disloyal and a traitor, and I had no clue. I never had a voice and he did not have ears to listen and believe the good in me, so this became the life for my poor husband having to put up with all my faults and bad habits.

From that day on, I could do nothing right. All was my fault, and my poor husband had to put up with me. I never fit in and never would. I guess I should look back and be happy they spent so many hours badmouthing me and putting me down. I must have been doing something right. I never heard that from them, just how I had ruined his life and all the misery and heartache I caused him and his family. It's strange how some people gain power and strength in destroying someone else or putting her down. I can be kind for so long and after trying and trying to get situations resolved and not being heard, then I can be the bitch on wheels. It takes a lot to get me that way, and I usually have a valid reason to go to that extreme. I do not like myself that way, but unfortunately that's how I got heard. How sad I had to go that direction to have a voice and be heard. Why should one have to beg for professional services when one is paying for them—they are not free, and one is expected to pay for services and not receive them. Give them to me for free, and then I can understand why the services do not work.

My devoted husband and father would keep our son out on school nights, pimping him for pool, and yet I was the sick, irresponsible one. I would call him to get our son home as a school night, and I was the nag and called too many times. I was branded the crazy, irresponsible one, yet I was getting our son to school, activities, and his full-time job. I was the psycho, demented woman. Family, friends. and strangers believed my husband and the stories he told. When I would stop taking my medications and had a voice, he was bad-mouthing me to anyone who would listen that I was off my meds. Control, control. He didn't want me and would make sure no one else would have or want me. He relied on lies and deception, and people ate it up. In order to see my son, I had to go to parenting class. This was as low an insult he and family and lawyer could give me, but I wanted to see my son and would pay the price to see him. Yet I was the one feeding him, getting him to school, doing the homework fighting the toothbrush battle, and reading to him at night. This was the pain and sacrifice I made to see my son with my mental illness record hanging over my head. The feeling of defeat I felt to be ordered to go to a parenting school while I was the one all along being the parent. I will never understand this or the hurt and betrayal a loved one can inflict on their loving partner. I put my pride and pain aside so I could see my son. If only I had been a bad mother like all believed.

I was only the designated driver and never a drinker. You think I'm scared of hell; try driving home with a drunk husband telling you he is going to end your life as he shoots a loaded gun as you are driving seventy miles per hour down a back road. The bullet whizzes by your head out the open window. I never lost control of the vehicle, and we both made it home safely. Who was the sick one in the relationship? I ask again: who was the sick one? I never lost control of the vehicle, and to this day I look back and wonder how we both survived.

Have you had a gun pointed at you? Has it gone off? I pray you do not have this experience. I took the blame all those years, but he was the ill one the whole time and had drinking issues gambling and women issues. Unfortunately, being the loyal, loving, devoted, and trustworthy wife got me all this -doing as he said and not as he did.

Between him, his family, and the doctors, they broke me. My spirit, humor, and trust all suffered, but I rose again, and I did it pretty much on my own with my faith and a few good friends and family members. Yes, my husband put me in the mental home. I begged and cried and pleaded with him not to leave me there. He basically put an innocent victim in there to suit his own selfish needs and continue the control and beat down of his wife.

I know how a young child feels when a teacher has branded him as a troublemaker who won't make it through school: future teachers automatically treat him that way. I was now considered crazy and a psycho bitch; he and his family made sure of that. Do you know how it feels to go to a doctor and he or she has already seen your reports from previous doctors who did more harm than good? Instead of dealing with you objectively, they tell you are lonely and nothing is wrong with you. This is what happened to me. They were the professionals. I had no voice, and I almost had to die to be heard. I had been branded by one doctor due to my husband's tale; no one asked for my story. The doctors were treating me from what my husband—-the perfect Catholic, God-fearing man from an influential family—told them.

Where was my voice? All someone had to do was ask me and listen, but I was branded weak, crazy, lying psychotic—-you name it. Meanwhile, behind the scenes I was the one keeping the family together, but when his mommy spoke, my husband jumped. Again, these were active members of the church. God is all forgiving, and yet some of the most judgmental people are the ones sitting in the pews. I believe in God, and my faith has gotten me through so much. I was one of those who never missed a Sunday in church, and I still love the feeling of walking into a church. I cannot always say much for the community, though, which is sad. God is our judge, and I believe most of us are doing the best we can, but we need to learn to be more forgiving as our God is.

I remember waking up at 2:00 a.m. and not finding my husband in bed with me and calling his phone just to see where he was. I was found to be in the wrong, too controlling and demanding and a nag for wanting to know where my husband was while I slept and our son was in his own room asleep. Again, I had to go to parenting classes thanks to my husband's lies and deceit. I was considered to be the destructive parent; and people believed the bs my husband preached. I had to go to parenting classes even though I was putting our son to bed while he was in the bar and sleeping around.

I marvel in delight that I still consider myself a warrior, fighter, and child of God after all the lies and mistreatment. After being the bad guy for more than thirty years, here I am still apologizing and taking the blame when most of the time it really is not my fault and never was. Have you ever had your spirit and light taken away? I have still never done a recreational drug and am not a big drinker. I have let loose a couple of times in my life; it's no wonder I felt like a caged animal. Maybe I should have become a nun. I loved being a mother and wife. I would have eight little boys over for dinner and to spend the night. I loved it, and at the same time I knew they were in a safe environment. No, I was not into little boys that way either. I am sure if my husband could have gotten me on that, he would have.

So unfortunately, marriage was not my safe zone—more of a war zone. When no longer had a voice and instead became the passive shadow with no voice, all was well. Our marriage was supposedly saved by a therapist and my husband, who ganged up on me. Of course, our marriage was considered to be strong when I became the passive *yes, sir, whatever you want, sir* submissive wife. Our marriage was saved by the therapist—no, I would say by me as I gave up my voice to keep my son and husband. I took my vows seriously.

When my husband got cancer, his family sent me a book to remind me not to leave and instead to be his wingman. My vows were in sickness and health. My girlfriend said I should have burned the book, but I was stupid and just put in our bookcase. Sadly, if I had been the ill one, he would have been gone the first month. He threatened throughout our marriage to leave, and during fights he often left. I never knew whether he was coming back or not. The actions of mature adult? No thought of me or his son in the room. He sure had the courts fooled, though; he would have gained full custody of our son in a divorce due to my mental state. There are very few cases where the woman loses, but I would have, and that was not right. Yet when we were separated, he was in the local bar while our son was with his mother doing all the things I had done as his mother The damage and scars he and his family did to me and my son are deep. I always wanted more children, but now I know why God only gave me one—and I loved him above all. I would have taken a bullet for my husband or my son. I almost did take a bullet from the one I pledged my love to. What goes on behind closed doors is always a different story than what the public see. My issue is I over-love—sad but true.

Another stigma tied to my mental illness concerned my work away from home. Two companies used my mental health as an excuse to fire me. When I look back, this was caused by jealousy and insecurity of the women work force. They saw me as a threat.

In the first case, I hired an attorney and actually won. All I asked was to keep my job. It basically boiled down to jealous women now that I look back, and I was a threat because my life was too good The women complained I was not doing my job, yet students were coming in and asking to speak with me, and I was called a princess. This was while I was on welfare and a single mother raising a son on my own, in addition to being considered a minority; all the odds were against me. The department was run by a women; for her to allow this to go on is sad. There should have been a compromise instead of having to hire an attorney to take down the lies that I was not doing my job by some insecure and vindictive women. What is the saying? Keep your friends close and your enemies closer.

In the second case, the bosses made me to go counseling and pretty much used my situation against me. This also was started by other insecure, vindictive women—basically, evil women. How sad that women go against each other and do not support each other but instead tear each other down. I think men are often easier to work with. At this point, I found out my husband had cancer, and the bosses gave me the option to resign or be fired. My husband told me to let them fire me. It is sad how women can be to punish you for doing your job and doing it well just because you are perceived to be a threat and one that women cannot deal with. Also, I really had no desire to climb the corporate ladder by bed or legitimately through hard work. I do not want to be that women fighting to keep her position by playing dirty against other women. How do they sleep at night? Well, easily when they have no conscious and are ruthlessly evil in nature. Some women unfortunately fit all the stereotypes out there about them. So they go to church to ask for forgiveness for destroying someone. How many times do they follow this cycle and still get ahead. I guess it's true that evil women get ahead and always win. How can a woman in this type of power and position allow this to happen to other women working for them?

What is wrong with this picture? How sad is it to have to hire an attorney when all you want to do is keep your job and make a living. They play the family business card but use computers to be dishonest and not have to pay someone for making them money. I thought a strong work ethic was a good thing. Who knew?

Mental illness is serious and sadly has been held against people who used to be kept in the closet. It is a disease and not to be taken lightly, but it also is not to be used to over-drug you, and you as the patient need to have a voice and be heard. I was misdiagnosed many times, and my husband's and the doctor's response was to up my medicine and pretty much make me a walking zombie, with no feelings, no voice, and no emotion. All they wanted from me was a *yes, sir* answer and to do as I was told. I fought back. I needed to be heard—*me*, not my husband telling my story and never letting me go to an appointment alone. By going together to each appointment, we showed a united front as if he cared. Actually, it was his control and a move to keep the meds coming. So how did these highly educated doctors not see through his deceptions? I have often been told I should be a therapist, and I took a lot of psychology classes in my time. I have the ability to see through such deceptions. I also helped young teens in a treatment home. Thank goodness I believe those young ladies were in a safe environment, unlike my situation. Yet I had no voice and no say. How can that be when I'm the patient. I learned to stay silent to keep the peace in my life, both marriage and overall. I was my husband's shadow, and that was the way he wanted it.

As I indicated above, I almost had to die before my a doctor and his ego who thought I just wanted attention and male company would take my situation seriously. Meanwhile, he kept wanting me to have appointments and said I was getting better and better. He labeled me as a problem because I questioned him and his diagnosis. I did not have asthma as he diagnosed, but he was spreading untruths to his partners. We as patients do not have the right to question and disagree with a doctor as they are educated? Because of my mental illness record, written by those doctors with my husband's guidance, I almost died—and no, it was definitely not asthmas but required two throat surgeries. It is thanks to the higher power and angels that it was not my time. Is it worth it to ruin someone over the need to be right? Or the need to prove a point? I have nothing against doctors or teachers—both tough fields—but we need to have a voice and be heard. Open the mind before jumping to conclusions. Please? I ask this of each and every person reading this book.

Should these records be available to anyone and everyone and be used against someone? To be branded, and what if it is not true? Who are these physicians playing God? There are of course the good along with the not-so-good just like anything in life.

Why am I telling you my story? For fame success? No, because I want you to know there is nothing wrong with you as a person, and it is an illness. Mental illness can be treated, and you will and can be OK. I still struggle with this and what it has done to me, and I cannot get over the idea that I have done something wrong and so am being punished, but why? I used to believe it should be left in the closet as it showed weakness and failure as a person, that I should not have failed with all the blessings and family and support I had in my life.

This should never have been the way we thought about mental illness. Mine was not as severe as a lot are, and I was definitely misdiagnosed and fell into a cycle controlled by my husband and the doctors. It was his way of controlling me and not facing life. When he figured out who I was all those years he had me in his life—unassuming and giving love, standing by him through all his shit and always there for him through the good and the bad, truly loving him and taking my vows seriously—it was too late. And in that instant, the truth hit him. He appeared so strong and authoritative and in control, yet he was easily manipulated and controlled by his mother and close friends, and always against me. In the end, he may have been the ill one but clever enough to keep me in his world. He did not want anyone else to have me. In the background, he was drinking more than I even knew in order to face his demons, and despite all the hell he put me through, I was always there for him. Loyalty can be a good thing, but I take it seriously and do not have a vindictive or vengeful nature.

Even though I had doctors and some supportive members in my family, I never felt more alone that during all my appointments.

My husband was there, and I was never given the chance to tell how I truly felt. He kept me silent and under his control. When I had a voice, there were passionate arguments, and neither one of us wanted to back down. I usually did back down to keep the peace. My son remembers the best part of his life as no fights. Those were the times I was overmedicated and silent.

What a battle I had and still have to get all out of the mindset that I was never that depressed, suicidal, or unable to get out of bed. Thanks to God, I realize the problem was mostly controllable crying and, I believe, postpartum depression, but my husband kept it going through the years. When he passed, I broke the mold. Think about how that went over with my in-laws after twenty years of being labeled crazy, mentally unstable, and a lost cause. It did not go over well, but I was no longer in his control and broke out on my own.

During my widowed years, I have been played and have learned some hard lessons. Despite my life and age, I still had a naivety for life. I laugh as I remember running into an old friend, and he asked how many times I had been married since my husband died. I could say not once. I was still alone.

I got caught up online with an unknown person and to this day have no clue who he was or is. I guess he or she kept me content, and I had someone to chat with. I will never underhand how I fell into this situation. It is so unlike me, a stable reliable person despite my mental illness labels. I never met this person and have no clue who he or she was, but I learned a valuable lesson that kept me from getting into worse situations.

The dating sites were not a good fit for me, and all the bizarre things that could happen did. I had only one date. I know there are good men out there, and maybe some crossed my path, but they didn't give me a chance or I didn't give them a chance. Concerning the total rejection of me by so many, I thank God I didn't let all the rejection and hate get to me. I have love and faith in me, so it didn't affect me except to continue on my decision to be single. How can someone not love herself and be strong-willed and stay in control without getting into self-destructive behavior. I was asked for money, sex, and you name it.

I wish to this day I had never got on the dating sites but many have good luck with them, just not me. A woman can only take so much rejection, and honestly, I am happy and content as I am. I love dancing, companionship, and all that, but it looks like those things are not in my cards, and so be it. I thank God I am fine being alone. Do I get lonesome? Maybe, but not enough to go looking. I thank whoever my online person was, and during COVID-19, he or she kept me safe and home. I do not think it helped me except to keep me company, and at this point after all the rejection by so many, I have no desire to let anyone in, but at one point I had hope of a second chance. Maybe this is the way of God and the universe to keep me single. I know I can be content and happy alone. I have had two previous stalkers and thankfully both were apprehended by law abiding police force and kept me safe to live another day from unknown tormentors. This sicko keeps me home, but as long as I don't leave, all is well in my world. I am not vengeful, but I pray he meets his justice. This is my third stalker. I wonder how I can leave my home and will I open my heart again? It's looking doubtful right now. So be it. I think my unknown online person may have gotten some of my heart, but sadly I never met or will meet him. I won't have any rebounds from this situation, and I envy those who can move on so quickly in matters of the heart. Life would be so much easier for me if I could do the same.

My son told me six months after his father died that he was fine with me dating. That was far from my mind, and I was not ready. I may never be after all the bizarre things I have had to deal with since my husband's passing. I thank God I am not afraid to be alone, and how does that work in the mental illness world. To be content and happy alone? Is that a class of mental illness I don't know about? Is there a medicine or doctor for this? I have lost many friends and family due to my fight to be who I am and to stand by what I believe in. I also would not let them label me now that I was trying to get my voice back and use it. I lost a good friend, and she ended up in a relationship like mine, and I saw the light fading from her and knew she was going down the road I had been down. I kept trying to be there for her, but she eventually closed me out for good. We would make plans, and she would cancel at the last minute. Oh how well I knew this behavior! I would make plans and all of a sudden, I had to do something for my husband and would have to cancel. I remember that world so well.

To have a voice again and wanting to be heard. Someone is still trying to destroy me and make me appear crazy and irrational, but *why*? What have I done that is so horrible? No one deserves what is and has been done to me. Unfortunately, I don't even know who my enemy is or what I have done that was so wrong. I simply chose to keep fighting and wanting to be a part of life.

I had family and a therapist take my son and grandchildren away and did not know why. Because I would not seek out help when I did not really need it? By bringing all the untruths to the light? I continue to pay for not going along with the stories my husband and family spread about me. For going above all the lies and deceit I lived for so many years. Here I am still paying. I thank my God and angels and my family and friends that have stood with me through all this.- My main point in all this is keep your voice and speak; don't be afraid. Life is short. Keep fighting. We all have our battles, and we all do the best we can with what has been given to us.

Why I was given this journey I will never know, but I just keep putting one foot in front of the other. As if this weren't enough mental anguish, someone continues to try to terrorize me, and I can only guess that it is to make me look crazy. Why? That was so many years in the past. If I can help one person, this was worth it, If only I had had an ally back then. My mother was there, but my husband had all the control and used it. I had to beg to get out, and it was not a safe place. To be frank, I think my husband needed time to get himself out of trouble and I was asking too many questions.

As I look back, he seemed to be independent but would take anyone's word over mine. Still, I stood by him through thick and thin. I never gave him any reason to doubt me, even when he put the house in my name—and what did I do when he was ready to have back in his name? I willingly did it. I had a girlfriend tell me I was a fool after all the hell he put me through, and yet I was the loyal and loving wife as always. So be it. Also, she told me I was mainly a maid for him and his family: cook, dishwasher and house cleaner. I was bad-mouthed by all for it. They said I was being paid for my work—another fable made up by the relatives. How does one who is always her husband's shadow and looking out for the best for him be so bad-mouthed and put down? His family would look me in the eye and knife me in the back. They are a cliquey bunch, and if you don't play by their rules, you don't fit in. They put up with me only because I was his wife. I think he loved me in his own way or the way he was raised, but I don't consider his love a worthy, true love, and all the time he was working on getting rid of me due to all the demands being made by his family and another woman, I am sure. Maybe that was my fault; he always said I couldn't handle the truth, but the truth is all I ever wanted. By the time he realized what he had in his life or who I truly was without the lies of all those around him—his supporting, loyal, and loving wife standing up for him—it was too late.

Do you know how I ended up in the mental intuition? My husband said we were going to get help for my crying. I remember walking into the building and my husband greeting the doctor. I was left alone on the bench while the two of them went into the office to talk with the door closed. –I, the patient, was left alone in the hall on a bench, considered to be a danger to myself but left alone and nothing happened. When the door opened an eternity later, I remember watching my husband walking down the hall, never looking back at me or giving me a kiss, just walking with his back to me. I was crying and pleading. "Why are you leaving me? What have I done? Please don't leave." But he did leave, seemingly without a thought.

He never came once to see me where he committed me—not once. He never called to check on me. I finally told my mother I was going to run like a convict and fugitive after being raped in this hellhole of a *safe place*. I stopped taking my medications so I could stay awake, but the professional staff were able to figure that out. I could not release myself, my parents could not release me, and finally after my parents agreed to pay for my stay, my husband arranged my release. What a loving and wonderful man I married. It took me years to sleep, and the nightmares are still present. My husband who supposedly so loved and protected me put me in a hellhole.

The final straw was when a therapist and his family took my son away from me. I will never understand, and again it was presented as my fault. In all honesty, I guess I am one who loves too much. I do not give my heart away easily. People around me fell in and out of love all the time. I had a girlfriend in one relationship and the next month in another one. I wonder if that might be easier when I look back, but I have no complaints. I am who I am and was always have been, and that is fine. Here I am still alone after being widowed, and part of me always wanted to grow old with someone. That was part of marriage and being in a relationship, and it is the way I was raised. I never saw my future as growing old alone, but I will face that like I do and everything else I have had to face. That is what I have been dealt, and I will play it out.

At one point maybe two to three years after being widowed, I was excited to maybe meet someone and dance again, dine out again, and have a companion, but after rejection after rejection and feeling like a weirdo on the dating sites or being wanted just for sex or money, I figured there was definitely something wrong with me. I decided I was better off alone: I expected too much, and a relationship was not in my cards. I started to wonder if maybe my husband and his family were right, that I was a failure and really didn't fit into this society after all.

To be mentally ill, you are not supposed to be reliable, trustworthy, or dependable to get things done. You aren't supposed to be able to get out of bed or have a sense of humor or succeed—yet I did and have unless I was overmedicated. Then I couldn't think and only wanted to sleep. This is not the cure for mental illness, being drugged so you can't function in daily life and misdiagnosed to the purpose of your husband's desire to keep control of you.

Here is another example of how he controlled me, and sadly, I had to find this out from another source. My husband had overdrunk and wanted pleasure in the bedroom. Of course, I was in no mood for any kind of sexual endeavor due to his toxic mood and state. I pushed him away, and he fell into the couch. Little did I know he had broken ribs, and I then was accused of being the one who broke his ribs. I really did not think I had pushed him that hard, and he fell into our couch in a sitting position. He let me live with that lie and told others that I had broken his ribs; even to this day, my son believes I did. My husband took that to his grave and held that over my head all the years of our marriage. Later, I learned it was a bar fight over a woman, while I of course I was under the impression he was working late as usual. my workaholic husband, or so it seemed or he portrayed.

This makes me wonder what else I had done and had no clue of doing. It is too late now, and I will never know. Although he is gone, this horrid history still follows me. Life goes on, yet I continue to pay for untruths and things I really didn't do. To think I cried days and nights that I had broken his ribs—what was wrong with me? How could a loved one do that to her significant other? How? I thought I would never fit in this world. I remember a family member telling someone I had scars, but they were minor for the few short years you were involved with him and his family. My scars are many, and I feel like a young calf being branded and carrying through the years under the control of others.

My current tormentor keeps this fear alive, and I may never move forward again or look to a relationship. Why? This is the universe and God's way to continue to destroy me. I ask again for what? Truth?

There are two sides to every story. I want to get mine out there, and if this helps one person in the world of mental illness, it is worth it? To know they are not alone? I still do not know the vendetta this creep has or why he or she is bound to bring about my destruction. I pray. I continue to fight, keep my spirit, my will, and my truths, and pray for justice to be served—probably not by the legal system, but maybe with God's hand or karma. I am not vengeful, but I want justice done to this individual in such a bad way. It drives me each day against an unknown assailant. I keep hope alive for justice—minor or detrimental— is all too much to ask? There are so many other tragedies in life and major and so undeserving. It makes me question whether or not there is a God? Yes, there is, though I often don't understand his way. This is not God's way or the universe's way; this is the way of a simple sicko in our sick world.

My son gave my mother-in-law credit for raising him for one month when we were separated, yet my husband had a fifth-grade reading level, so was I really a failure as a mother? Family, society, and parenting class I had to attend to see my son. This shows what power, money, and greed can do a small person. So I paid and paid and continue to do so.

Do you know what is feels like to be told for more than twenty years that there is something wrong with you, that you are sick and going to fail? I was told this day after day, and yet here I am, so was I so insecure, clingy, and needy and the loser that I was made out be? After all those years, here I am, still fighting alone against all odds and with loved ones close by. I had my spirit broken, and I rose again. I had my faith and a few good friends and family members. Looking back, I think my husband was not my friend and thrived on beating me up and making him feel more powerful, strong, and the boss. Some people need to dominate to remain powerful; by hurting others, they build themselves up. How can people not see the truth? Or did they see it but decide it was easier to point the finger at me and enjoy my putdown.

Then there were the ones who said I have or had everything going for me, so how could I let this happen? Need attention? How all those years did I remain strong, depending on myself and my faith and my few close friends and family? There were times when I was struggling that I went outside into nature. I still do: it doesn't cost anything.

I never wanted to be in that mental prison that will haunt for the rest of my life. I have nightmares to this day over my mistreatment when I was supposedly in a safe place. Instead, I was in hell, and not a hell made by me. While a loved one put me in there and left me, never once looking back or coming to see me, his lies and mistruths are what put me in there with the doctor's help. He thought I would never know the lies he wove. This is someone I shared my life with and thought I would grow old with. Only when he was dying from cancer did he truly see me and realize what he had had beside him all those years that took for granted, misused and treated like a doormat.- As I said before, by than it was too late All those years of deceit, late nights when he claimed to be working, lies about having a daughter he swore to me was not his— yet everyone else knew she was. How could I be so blind? I gave my word, love, and vows to this man. I was old school, and that meant you stood by your man. He controlled my world, and as long as I made peace and did as I was bid, all was well in our universe.

Right before he became ill with cancer, he started acting like the man who had wooed me in our younger years, and we started to have a marriage of doing things together and being a true couple. Whoever poisoned him about me maybe was no longer in control, and he was learning to look to me as a partner within marriage as it should be. Sadly, it was too late, and time was short and took him when things were finally going in our favor again.

My next journey was to keep him alive, and that I did; we made it almost four years battling cancer and all that goes with it. It's too bad that cancer had to bring us together, make us closer, and force him to have to rely on me and listen to me. I had a voice again, and he was able to see how much I truly had loved him all the time. We were together 24/7, and I had a voice. I do not think he had the strength or will to fight, even if he didn't believe I was right.

His doctor said through all four years, he never heard me say I was right, even though I was. He said I was my husband's lifeline, looking out for his good and health and keeping him alive. I got him to all appointments, made sure he had his meds and chemo, and protected his life. It was a full-time job.

The doctor who had the utmost respect and admiration for me was the doctor my husband wanted in charge of his care. He told my husband, "Look next to you and see her— *really* see your wife. My wife would never let an opportunity go by without reminding me that she was right."

How can life and family go so wrong? Again, I know he loved me only as he knew how to love and was raised. His love came at a high cost Maybe I had read too many romance novels or watched too many movies. What started out so perfect took a horrible twist down the wrong path.

The other mistake I made from being naïve concerned a couple who were friends of ours. We did a lot together, but things ended in tragedy. We all went to a holiday party, as we often did, only the night took an unexpected turn. While we were at the party, my husband's attention was focused elsewhere, which was not surprising, and he was not one to check to see if I was OK or needed another beverage. He looked out for himself. While I sitting at a table with maybe five other people, I felt a hand on my knee and was surprised, so I looked up. The husband of the couple had his hand on my knee and was smiling. I got up and walked away in great shock and astonishment. This could not be happening. I minded my own business and stayed away from him. When we got home, my husband said I was awfully quiet, and I decided to tell the man I thought was my best friend what had happened. Boy, was that a mistake and one I never repeated. He pretty much called me a liar and said our male friend would never do that or put me in that type of situation. He said I was a storyteller, just jealous of the attention he was getting and so I had to make up a story. He said the situation was all my fault and I must be desperate to get his attention, needy and clingy. I think he contacted our neighbor and apologized for my rude behavior and said it would not happen again. Here we go again! It was my fault and who would want me? He was stuck with me, poor hubby of mine. How did he end up with such a loser? Being who I was, I never saw a friend doing that to me or to his wife, who was one of my best friends. This was not my world.

Then I went from this episode to a close family member telling me to open my eyes and asking if I noticed that man looking at me and smiling. No, I didn't, and after so many years of feeling ugly and undesirable, I wouldn't notice that someone was looking at me in interest. Did I have a mark on my face?

Something wrong? Then I had another close family friend tell me I attracted the wrong kind of men. I was not even looking. How could I attract anyone's attention. I faded and blended in. I was told I would have to be hit on the head for someone to show interest in me.

It was the result of years of feeling like a wall flower, I guess—I don't know—and the one time I tried to make an attempt I was rudely rejected. I need to open my eyes after being rejected and rejected by so many through all the years. What is out there for me? When I took a chance, the door was slammed. When I didn't, was there something wrong with me? Maybe my world is safer and does not hurt when I don't try. How can someone so depressed fake laughter, be alone and content. Laughter is not a magic pill. Belief in myself and loving myself despite all my scars and failures, and focusing on the blessings I have is what I strive for. I have won a few battles and lost many battles, and I still have hope and faith.

Open your eyes, they say. They? Who are they? Do you think our world is great anymore, with all the sacrifices our veterans and military people made and things they gave up for our country? Are we still proud? Where is the neighbor, where is the handshake, and where is wanting only the good for others instead of the desire to break them make them suffer and take their spirit? Do others not deserve what they have? What about all the work and sacrifice they made? Who are we to judge?

I believe God is our ultimate judge in the end, and he is all-forgiving. What a great way to look at the pain we as people put him through. What right do we have to do that to a person? Yet we do that with words as well. I may over-love, but I would have sacrificed my life or taken a bullet for my husband or son or other family members. I have a loyalty that if you earn, you can always count on. I don't expect something, and I will give without receiving. I still believe in good, even though I have scars to prove life isn't always good. Yes, I may be the mental one, and my husband put me in that hellhole. Thank God that place is no longer in business to destroy others as they seem fit in order to turn a profit.

When does hiding your medications become such a bad thing. Is it any wonder he put me in there? His strategy worked, though. He controlled me the rest of my life, and if I had left him, I would have lost my son. How many mothers lose their children in a divorce? Not many. He made his point, and I have lived with it for years with his reinforcements, his family and friends and society, who went along with the deceit and the false reports doctors wrote. What did my husband do that was so bad to ruin me and keep me in tow? He did not want me but didn't want anyone else to have me. How ironic to finally figure this out while he was dying, to realize that the family member he trusted and listened to was weaving tales of deception. that what started out so happy and wonderful could have continued that way with normal ups and downs of life. Instead, it became the extreme roller coaster he had us on.

I was the kind of girl you take home to mother, so what happened to change that? I had a friend ask me if I myself? Of course I do, and I respect myself and love myself. I don't fit in our world. I won't make excuses, and I don't judge others—that is not up to us. We all will all meet our maker in the end. That will be the final word. I often think people don't like themselves when they do destructive things to themselves. Life is tough, but it also has much happiness in addition to the sadness and loss. We are all doing the best we can in an unfair world.

I think my husband loved me in the way he learned to love growing up, but he was also listening to many voices and always thought the pasture was greener on the other side. As I stated above, by the time he realized what he had with me, it was too late. It is sad how that works. I don't know if my scars will ever heal. After his death. I was tormented by the unknown stalker who has made my life hell basically. Again, I ask if you know what it feels like to have some unknown invader coming into your home and helping themselves to family heirlooms and treasures that I cannot replace. I know these are just material possessions, but I look at something from someone and remember who they were and the memories we shared.

Do you know what it feels like to find stool samples and grease on your carpet and have no clue who this home invader is? Do you know what it feels like to have your home your safe place away from this crazy world to be invaded, taking that security away from you? The feeling of never being safe again—who has the right to do that to you? To be thought of as a joke and have no control over your own home. To be at the mercy of someone and not know who this creep is or what you did to deserve this. This is *your own home*!

So what do you do? Stay home and be thankful being alone and telling yourself that home is not such a bad thing because it is away from the drama of the world? I love life. How can someone who loves life be so depressed and on the verge of paranoia? Well, who wouldn't be paranoid after being stalked? Who wouldn't be looking over her shoulder? You imagine him time after time again coming into your home, robbing you, sitting on your couch, and invading your personal space. Everyone said I needed a therapist. Can they catch this creep? The police could not help me without a picture of the jerk, and I couldn't count on security. I paid my bills, but it never worked. How the hell does someone win this type of situation? I not a runner and this jerk definitely has no conscience, so how can I win? I am stubborn, maybe crazy, but this is my home, and no one has the right to torment me.

I lost many friends who said it's only stuff, but it's mine, and as I said, many of those material possessions have cherished memories associated with them. I may need therapy now. I don't want to let anyone in my home and have a fear of leaving my home. Do you know what it feels like to walk into your home and check the closets and wonder if it will be your last day on earth? Do you wonder what you did to be punished so badly?

Thanks to this unknown creep, I have issues and scars, but therapy won't help, only justice, and the police can't even help. So I fight my losing battle alone.

I am glad someone is laughing and enjoying their domination and violation of me. When they took my wedding albums, I knew than it was a sign I was to be alone, and I have not to this day had a physical relationship with another man. I do not think it's in my future. This must be God's way of protecting me. I think I still have a heart. Someone came into my life maybe a year after my husband died, and we were in constant touch but never met, and yet I let him in and even gave him money with promises of payback. I never was paid back and learned that his promises were all lies but in a good way. I was home and safe, As a realist, I will never understand this connection and to this day really don't know who he was.

I got off all social media and stopped the dating sites due to many sexual offers or people wanting money. Also, I was not used to the attention of men and women contacting me. It was easier to put walls up and protect myself. You can be kind for so long, and then you are the doormat. If you get angry or make waves, then you are spoiled and a bitch.

The truth of the matter is this is a world where most people don't care and everything is just about them. It's a sue-happy and greedy world. I have lists of missing items, but I'm considered the crazy one. I'm told it is all in my head. A friend asked me if I felt vulnerable and if I needed the support of someone. No, I really felt like I never had the support of my husband, so I was used to handling things on my own. He pretty much threw me to the wolves and never had my back. So this situation just made me want to fight, and I prayed this creep would come when I was home so I could who was tormenting me and face him eye to eye. What a coward. Total coward and loser.

God says things happen for a reason. I do not know what his reason was, and my only conclusion was to stay single. I don't think this is the work of God or the universe, and no good has come from this torture and destruction of me. Even though I prayed and thought I wanted a second chance, that apparently was not to be. Luckily, the good thing about my fantasy relationship was it kept me loyal to an unknown individual and really was not looking for a relationship. I am not normal, and most people fall in and out of love easily. I do not. When my girlfriends were all dating, I was thrilled my parents told me I had to wait until I was sixteen, and I really was not normal in the boy-crazy way. You almost must knock me alongside the head to get my attention, and I am still liking and staying in my own world a lot. It's safer, and I am happy.

As a realist, how could I have connected with an unknown person. I know he was fraudulent because every time I tried to force a meeting, either on FaceTime or Zoom he never agreed. I know it was lies and deceit, but it was easy and did not change my life. As a realist in a fantasy relationship, sadly, I was content, and when I asked for more I was refused, so I knew it was deceitful, but with my previous experience, I was content to let it be. When this person ended it with me. I cried. I felt like a fool because I never met the person yet he had such a hold on me. Oh, well, another player having fun at my expense. I almost envy women who can have one-night stands and continue on.

I may not be normal, but I need to have my heart involved, though I'm not a prude or a nun. I have been told I am reserved or cold, but that is not true. Maybe I am too selective. Do I miss companionship, handholding, and intimacy? Of course. And if I invite you in, the invitation is sincere and not easy for me to do. Have I invited someone into the intimate part of my life? Not many. I have been told I'm too selective and have too much self-control. I'm not here to judge, and God will be my judge in the end. We all do best we can.

I was married a long time and never cheated, and I am proud of that. It's not easy to move on from a committed long-term relationship with one man. It took me a long time to realize I was single and could date. We all deal with grief in our own way: there is no right or wrong; each to his or her own. Then when I did start to date, it was not a good experience, and my excitement of maybe getting a second go around faded. A good friend asked me how many times I had been married after being widowed. I can laugh about this now: not once and only one date to my name. This new world of dating is not good for me. I wanted someone to dance with, eat dinner with, and see movies with—companionship   my hope of that happening quickly faded. I hear it's all in the timing and is more likely to happen when you are not looking. I really have not looked for a long time and hear if it is going to happen, it will happen. At this point, I am not sure I care anymore, especially since my first marriage was not what I had expected and hoped it would be. Even with a lifetime partner, how can you feel so alone and still committed to that person? Even though I loved him, sadly maybe too much, I may have expected too much. I do have many good memories, though there were many dark ones as well. He blamed me for all that was wrong in our life—all.

Have you ever been in a situation where you look like the bad guy but you were trying to maintain control of a situation without being attacked or possibly raped? Why does being widowed make you a target and seen as wanting sex all the time or as if you are available for a good time. When a woman calls to have a professional service provided in her home because she has no choice or cannot do that particular job herself, she can be vulnerable. In one situation, the serviceman would not leave until finally, after four hours of him not doing his job trying to get me to lead him to my bedroom, he finally suggested that I kiss him on the lips, have sex with him or agree to a date before he would leave *my* home. So being a kind woman gets you in this position and needy for the bedroom. So, trying to take control of the situation in my own home and not be put in a situation without an escape route, I told him I would give him a kiss on the cheek but I preferred to do so in the garage. I opened the overhead door so I would have a chance to run if so needed. This was my game plan. Being a flight attendant in the past in many different cities and different neighborhoods I learned how to watch my own back.

A woman should not have to worry in her own home. I wanted to maintain control of the situation, and no rape /sexual attempt occurred—thankfully. So did that make me a target, but who would believe me in this he said/she said situation? I am sure at least one of my nosey neighbors saw this situation, and the gossip grapevine started. I'm sure a whole different story was going around in the neighborhood. My strategy worked: he left, and I was left unscathed. But an hour or so later, I received a text from him as he had my phone number from the company he worked with. He was asking me on a date. I maybe should be flattered, but he was definitely not my type. Honestly, at this time I didn't know who the hell my type was. Not to ruffle feathers as I had to continue to do business with this particular company, I politely thanked him and said I was honored but not ready to date yet. Hell, I thought at that rate I may never be. I had arrived at the point where I did not want to let anyone in my home again and preferred my aloneness.

I remember hearing a story about a young woman who got friendly with her single, attractive male neighbor though casual visits and greetings in the hall. Then one day, she came home innocently with her groceries and the charming gentleman offered to help her carry her groceries into her apartment. This became a nightmare of hell when he raped her and violated her. She invited him in, so did she have this gruesome act coming to her? You be the judge. Was this her fault? She simply believed in the friendship of neighbors. I guess you just have to be careful who you open your door to. Unfortunately, when you need homework done, it's not always an option to refuse to let someone in.

I believe my husband loved me in his own way or the way he was brought up to. I think he was brought up in a family where love came at a cost and something would be expected in return. I think love should be given because you want to give it and that it should be free without strings attached. I love to give. Many times don't receive, but the feeling it gives me to see another smile or to receive a sincere thank you makes one life high for me. I have heard women say they had better get a good gift from their significant other for what they just did for him. Well, each to her own and no judgment, but shouldn't you do something for love and freely? Maybe you have expectations of helping him or her, standing by him or her, or working toward your shared goals.

You are in a relationship to support, respect, and work toward your life together. What better way is there than to be a part of or help your partner? But beware of becoming a doormat, always the giver and the other always the taker and expecting it. When you don't come through as you always have, then you are seen as spoiled, a brat, needy, and a bitch. You go out of character and you pay. If you put boundaries up with an *all his way* type of male, you will see which road you are going down and the power struggle that happens because you went out of your role as the giver, lover, and proper lady. Your voice will become faint, and so then ends the compromise.

Compromise to a male can be a sign of weakness and vulnerability, and the power struggle begins. Then if you both are stubborn, and you start setting boundaries or use the word *no*, angry arguments ensue, especially when you both are passionate. You get tired of picking fights and losing, so you start fighting constantly to get your voice back and to be heard. But you don't realize the damage that is being done. Finally, the more passive one starts giving in as she (or he) knows there is no hope for compromise and it's better to try to settle the turmoil without him walking out. Instead of talking as two rational adults, you start to fade into the shadows and lose your voice. You become passive and take the fault for all. Then, even though you are agreeing with what he decides and does, when something goes wrong, guess what? You are the bad guy and the fall guy.

I have a friend who was married for more than ten years and never had an argument or disagreement and thought she was in a perfect marriage, only to come home one day to her husband sitting at the table with divorce papers. What is the right way? Is there a right way? Marriage or a partnership is work and can be well worth it, I am sure. If someone tells me it is easy, I look at them to see if they are sincere. Does this make me a doubter?

I may never know at this point. One date and no one on the horizon, and I have no intention at this point of getting off my couch and back out there. Maybe this makes me a coward. Take more than thirty years in one relationship—how does one get her spirit back and her fight and passion for life? Think of what years of damage and destruction do to one's self identity, never feeling like you are good enough and always the failure, never getting over the feeling of always being wrong and apologizing. Sometimes I was not even sure what I was apologizing for. Was I really at fault every time?

If you enjoy life and you are not stoned or drunk, does that make you abnormal? I have only respect and admiration for those who overcome these types of addictions when life makes these outcomes an easy way out and easy to deal with. I remember my girlfriend and I giggling /laughing and someone saying "How high are you?" or "How much have you had to drink?" She would reply, "We are high on life." I always loved that answer, not an easy one in this world. So we were the weirdos for having innocent fun, and people thought there was definitely something wrong with both of us.

Or did we have a secret? For our senior kegger, we took bottles of apple cider, and were we a hit! What a great drink we had and were sharing. That was the innocence of youth and having clean fun without hurting anyone. Life is not easy; it forces us to make choices we may not have been happy we took. I do not judge others as I have not walked in their shoes, and there can be many reasons people do what they do. The end of each of us will be God's call.

What good does it do to beat people up for their choices? Most of us do the best we can do in the circumstances we are in. I do not think dishonesty, theft, rape, murders, violence, incest, or any other abuse is the right answer and should be dealt with through the justice system. Mental abuse can be just as damaging as the others, and words can cut knives in a person's soul. It might not show damage on the outside but instead is internal and hidden to others. Life is made up of many people, and there is no utopia.

There are two worlds: innocent people may pay for a lifetime, while some others do serious intense crimes and get off. I don't have the answer to this problem. Life is life and not an easy by any means. What happened to the good old days—handshakes, being a good neighbor, borrowing a cup of sugar, not worried about a Halloween treat having poison or razor blade hidden inside. We do the best we can and take different routes on our journey. We are all brought up differently in all different lifestyles.

Words can do damage; some are deserved, and some are not. Scars take time, and some heal and some do not. We have no clue what someone is going through in life. Does that give someone the right to treat you like shit? Is it true the evil and crooked get ahead? Some days I believe this and feel there is no justice for those and they get away with what they do. Other times I do not believe it. Why is being upfront and honest cause for jokes and speculation? Why does God allow bad things to happen if his way is so good? I guess if we don't know the lows from the highs, we may never experience true happiness.

Does it pay to work hard and try to survive when someone has you as a target and are not even sure what you did to be at their mercy and what you are paying for? Fighting against an unknown person and doing this on your own while you are depressed—why do I still have the power or will to fight this unknown jerk? Are they trying to prove I am mentally ill and unstable by invading my home and possessions and making me look like the crazy one? I have lists and lists of missing items. Do you know the money that this has cost me? I still have no clue who is doing this or why. Yet I'm the crazy one, and there is nothing wrong with this sicko doing this evil sick behavior to me? What is he doing to try to prove me crazy? Do I pee like a man and potty all over my bathroom floor?

When I took the stalker's gift of stool samples from my toilet to the police for DNA samples, the nice police detective had the gall to tell me they were mine and that I just was needing attention. To him, I was just a damn lonely widow—what is up with this stereotype? Where did it come from? It made me more committed to my fantasy relationship—safe at home— no sexual diseases, deceived but still focused on me. I may have helped this person as well. Who knows? It was easy and harmless. When he started asking for money, I gave a bit, but then that stopped, and so did the attention. I guess it came with a cost. Also, he would not meet me? What does that tell you? There was definitely something dishonest going on. I have no clue who he was and never will, But what does not cost in this world of ours? Love too can come at a cost, and sometimes the cost is high.

So is mental illness serious? Yes, of course, and it's as real as physical illness, as real as drug and alcohol addictions. Do I have the answers? No except to be your voice and ask questions. There are good doctors, and there are bad doctors as in any profession and situation, but be strong and listen to your instincts. The *magic pill* is not always the answer. .

God made me a warrior through my family upbringing and being on my own. I refuse to go down again. I remember when I could finally escape the mental institution. They said, "We will see you soon. It's normal to have a relapse." As I walking out but telling no one, I made a pact the myself there was no way in hell I would have a relapse. *No way in hell!* I would never be put in that situation again. I would run and disappear before that would happen again to me. Thank the Lord for my faith and for making me a warrior to keep fighting—not to mention that German trait of stubbornness I was given. If you do not trust your doctor, change! Ask questions, go with your instinct, keep fighting. Attitude is what counts in any situation.

Another thing I learned that could have led to my husband putting me in the mental institution was through my son, He had a really good friend and playmate. We did a lot together. His father was more involved with the son, while the mother was a career woman. There was nothing wrong with this picture either; that was just the reality of the situation. I had no clue that there was a problem, and we were all friends. I later heard through the grapevine that the wife had told my husband that her husband was leaving her for another woman and had his future wife in sight. Could my husband stoop that low and be that evil in his desire to keep me under control? This all happened at the same time he put in the institution. Also, there is such a thing called communication but he didn't ask me about it. I heard the couple did divorce. I don't really know what happened after that. My husband moved us to another state after my release, and again this was supposedly my fault. I really was innocent in this, and nothing happened to merit this kind of treatment. Could this be his revenge? For what? Something I had no clue was going on? Then his mother started buying what few clothes she did for me big and boxy. Was I that evil and suggestive? Did I ask for this type of treatment?

Another situation I'm still trying to figure out is how I became the bad guy in this situation. Did I get one of his old girlfriends pregnant? When we were engaged, he told me some woman claimed to be pregnant by him and denied it was his child She was greedy and slept around a lot, even with one of his friends after him, but he was the best potential husband and father material for her. I took in every word and believed him, of course. I also didn't want to be called and condemned like she was. Unfortunately, I had already had that type of treatment done to me. When the child turned sixteen, the mother and girl showed up, and I learned later he was secretly meeting her and her mother, even taking them out to his family and leaving me in the dark. His big excuse was I could not handle the truth. I think they had a DNA test done.

Actually, I could always handle the truth, but he preferred deceit and dishonesty. He kept me guessing and insecure and needy. His control led to my mental illness—or his claim of my mental illness. What a fool I felt; everyone in the family knew about this situation but me, his wife, his best friend who stood by him through this ordeal. Of course, it was my fault again.

Meanwhile, he's telling me the girl is not his and he has no intention of seeing her again. He did the same thing to her. He showered her with all his attention and love until he achieved what he wanted—his positive image—and when she didn't suit his purpose anymore, he closed the door on her and blamed me, his wife, for the fact that he wanted to stay married and didn't involve her in his life. Meanwhile, I'm the one sending birthday and Christmas cards, even signing them, so how could this be true? He was in control of the situation and, again, my fault, which caused me to be unstable and mentally ill. A magic pill supposedly could fix this, and I was the one in need of therapy.

Again, here I was: the bad guy. Still, I was doing more than surviving. I was doing more than just getting by. Later, after all his deceit that she was not his child, I learned that she *was* his child. I have total empathy for her and having to learn about his love and the cost of his love. I must have had some value, or he would have thrown me out in the cold as he did with those he did not want in his life or felt deserved to be in his life. But at what cost did I have to pay to be with him?

Oh, then let's bring in the money He put the house in my name during all this so we wouldn't t lose it. How sad when she turned twenty-one. Guess what? He asked me to put the house back in both our names. Being the loyal devoted wife, of course I did. Yes, maybe I was the mentally ill one. My close friend told me I was indeed crazy to do that, and why on earth would I do that again and still stand with him through all his hell, being considered the bad guy and of course at fault. Did he ever give me credit for being the loving, devoted, trustworthy wife that I tried to be who stood by him through all his shit and deceit? No, I did not. So many people didn't see this about him.

I remember going to a family wedding and being in the bathroom stall and hearing two family members talking about me. Of course I was the family joke. One of the women said, "So that's his crazy wife." "The other said, "Poor hubby." So I hid in the stall until they left, and then I made my exit. As I walking up the hall to go back to the reception, I met the groom and his best man. The best man was saying, "She doesn't seem crazy like the rumors have it." Usually, I would have retreated, but I kept going and said, "Yes, I am the crazy one!" That still makes me laugh. I should have done that years ago. They were the ones running up the hall, not me.

Another thing that made me seem mentally ill is I would avoid family functions as I did not want to be a target or be involved in all the drinking. So of course this contributed to rumors about my illness as I avoided family functions and get-togethers. I must be mentally ill. Actually, I didn't want to deal with the drama, malicious gossip, and putdowns. The family show front is not always what it seems and, in the bathrooms or corners, the truth comes out about who the family target is. Call it mental illness or something else. I must confess I used that to be able to stay home and not have to deal with family drama or be a target taking hits. Being looked in the eye and knifed in the back constantly is not a good thing. Neither is hearing how crazy you are and how all is your fault. *Poor hubby. Poor hubby.*

So do I believe in abortion? I believed in life as I believed in my marriage vows. Then circumstances happen, and you pay for your consequences. I really was not that experienced, and looking back, if he had been protecting, we would have done safe sex. Well, chemistry happens, and we were young and in love. I ended up expecting. Well, we decided to run away and do a Vegas wedding. I was all in.

Sadly, he listened to his family member telling him that was not a good idea, and he ended up calling and telling me it was not going to happen. We discussed our choices. That is when I first heard about the woman claiming to be pregnant who he said decided to trap him and take away his future. So against all my beliefs, values, and religion, I did the unexpected with his blessings. Of course, when the day came he couldn't get away, and a friend went with me. I should have seen this as a sign, but of course I didn't and should maybe have ended our relationship at that point. We were still engaged, and the wedding was still scheduled. Later, I heard he paid for this to happen. It was not true. I believe this is when I starting losing my identity and my voice. I think he blamed me through the years for this and led to the accusations that everything was my fault.

Would I do it again? This was not a form of birth control, and I was not an sexually active person. I followed through because I didn't want to be known for trapping him again and feeling the disdain he had for the women doing that to him and tarnishing his reputation. I would not be that women, but the friend who took me had gone through it, and her relationship fell through, and she ended up alone and childless. Why? I will never know the answer, and do I carry that guilt? Of course I do. Could I have let my child be adopted? No. I would never know if the child was safe or being abused, and that would have killed me in the end: the unknown.

Think of me what you will—it's your right. I will pay for what I did in the end, with God as my judge. I believe it was the situation and circumstances that led to me following through and when he failed to show as promised, and with my girlfriend beside me, I followed through. I have no excuses for what happened, and I live with it daily even though was years in my past, dead and buried it where I wanted it to stay. You can judge me, but I would never judge you, and it's a choice whether right or wrong. Could the guilt of what I did so against by beliefs and values help lead to my mental illness? It may have; the mind can do amazing things to a person. Also, I later learned he was under the impression the child was not his. It was. I was a flight attendant. I had a pilot tell me I was a door clicker and not a door opener. I guess I was not easy and opened the door for men/women and the grapevine knew? How I have no clue to this day, and why it was so important I will never know. It is no one else's business. Do you want to condemn me? I always think we don't know what we would do until we walk in that person's footprints.

We all make choices to the best of our abilities based on the circumstances and the judgments of our peers. Whether it's right or wrong, God is all-forgiving. I keep telling myself that. Unlike some people, I believe in this strongly with my faith. Have I paid? Yes. One thing it did is it forced me to be a hell of a mother, if I say so myself, and I was an excellent wife in that sense as well. I gave my motherhood my all and sacrificed all for my family. I maybe put too much faith in the family code and being a mother, I gave it my all and was there for as much as I could be—no excuses. I sacrificed me for my husband and son. I loved being a wife and mother. Family was so important; I maybe made it too important! I maybe gave it too much focus, but I have no regrets. I took joy in having eight to ten little men having a sleepover and making breakfasts for them.

I look back, and despite my mental illness, I gave it my best and my all with what I had to work with. Did I do the right thing? I will never know. Justice will be served to me with my God when my time comes, and I can live with that. Could I have let my child be adopted? No, the not knowing is by far worse for me with regard to the safety or unsafety of the child. Did I commit murder? Where was my soon-to-be husband? Again, this was my fault. Guilt? Of course, some adoptions are amazing and all goes well, but then there are the nightmare tales. Did I do the right thing? At the time I did think so. I also did not want to be accused of trapping my future husband. My previous love had it happen to him. I have no clue what was right or wrong. It was in the moment with my support system at the time.

Through all this, my husband let me take the blame. I told no one—not one soul. Little did I know he was spreading the word that it was all my fault. My husband, who was to be my confidant, was my own worst enemy and the persuadable family member. What do they say? Keep your enemies close and your friends closer. I think he loved me, but he punished me at the same time for the actions of both of us. I think that is when I went from the girl next door and to take home to Mom to the girl not to take home to Mom, and it stayed with me. But he had a daughter out there he was not claiming or supporting, and he was in her life for only a short time. I have no clue if he paid her off or if she got only my cards and funds I sent after getting approval from him to do so. What is the answer? I pray for her, and I know he cut her out of his life. Again, this was not my choice but I know I got the blame as I heard later. He had all the power, and if had I left, I would have lost my son. Who had the power? Funny how he could change stories to suit his needs and desires without consequences. Must be nice. He was able to get his way all the time. Meanwhile, I was paying the price.

Again, I go with my thought and prayers that God is all-forgiving. People are not.

Mental illness is real and not imagery. In my case, I think it was more forced and suited to fit another's needs and control of me. Why? I have no clue, and if I was such a bad problem to him, why did he stick it out all that time with me? Why did he listen to others and not to his heart or his feelings? Why was his aim so bad that New Year's Eve? I believe I have as many scars and issues as anyone, but in this relationship was I really the mentally unstable one, or should the roles have been switched?

I ask and beg others going through any mental illness: Please keep your voice, ask and ask questions, keep a strong attitude, and fight. It's not easy—and it is an illness—but keep fighting for life There is still a lot of light despite the darkness. Don't' go with the flow; question and be your own voice. Use your support system, but do not let them be your voice. They should stand by your side, hold your hand, and support you through this. No one should punish you for things that are not all your fault. Do not allow anyone to break your spirit and lose the fight for life. **Don't allow that.**

Medications are needed, but sadly they are often over–prescribed, and you can become a shadow and have no personality, no spark, and you just end up going through life without any emotions—a gray shadow. We cannot shine all the time, and I understand we need sadness to experience joy fully, but to be gray with no feelings and emotions as a result of being overmedicated is not the answer. To be so passive you sleep all the time and cannot function, void of all reactions. No, this is not the answer.

Please, doctors, understand that medicine is not always the magic pills; emotions are part of our humanness—don't make us robots, uncaring and void of words, thoughts, and reactions. A good cry is not always a bad thing. I understand it can become a problem if it happens constantly. My other thought is to ask you to talk to patients: hear their thoughts, listen to family members *but* in all treat the patients. *Listen* to them. They may know than you give them credit for.

Some stories sadly are true, and sadly some are untruths. Do not make us a number, and remember that you have a heart. We are all different, and we should not be treated the same. We are all unique with our upbringings, our lives, our experiences and culture. Remember that you may be the doctor, but we should be able to be heard. Don't take us lightly—we matter. We are human and not dollar signs, not another number in your day. Not an escape for family members and a source of control. Get to the heart of the matter. What I am asking is that you hear: hear the truths, hear the bullshit, and hear us to better the individual not make a voiceless vegetable.

Am I a doctor? No! Do I have the answers? I wish I did, but I do know my voice wanted to be heard for me and who I am, not who I was made out to be. Yes, people are judgmental, condemning, and cruel. As life is. Is this fair? No, but you have power, and you can make or break a person. Take more time to improve the situation.

What possessed me to write this and share my personal thoughts on this matter? The thought that if I could help one person who was at the mercy of another individual and the hands of the medical profession, it would be worth my effort. Of course, not all family members or doctors fall in that category, but sadly like anything, there is the good and evil—or just don't give a damn. Then patients can become a number or all about the dollar.

Be your voice, look for the light, and keep your faith, hope, and spirit alive. Don't get me wrong—it will not be easy. It is a battle, but what is a battle if you don't give it your all? Either way you did your best, and if you go down fighting, you will know you did what you could and held your own. We all do the best we can, and no one has the right to dominate and control a person. Mental illness is serious, and unfortunately, misdiagnoses are common. I have been blessed. I had my angels and faith and God to keep me going in addition to family I could count on when it looked like I was fighting a losing battle.

Never give up on yourself. You matter; love yourself. I can be my own worst enemy and overthink, but if you have me on your side, you will never have a more loyal and loving friend, wishing only the best. What I hoped to achieve was maybe peace of mind and a voice after all the mistreatment. Yes, I can still wear my heart on my sleeve, and that might not be a good thing, but to be totally controlled by another is not a good thing. Will I ever let anyone else in my life? At one time I had hope, but I don't think it is in the cards. Knowing that I never want to lose my voice again has kept me focused and has helped me work on my boundaries. –Yes, I can still be a pushover, and I have learned to forgive even if that person doesn't deserve my forgiveness, but as I once was told, holding on to anger and hurt only hurts you in the end.

My grandmother would always say it's never so bad that it can't be worse. Take that thought with you. Also, there is always light—even a small amount can weaken the darkness. It's not easy and can be a battle, but it's one that we can win. Sadly, our world doesn't make it easy when deceit is often an easier answer and gets you ahead. Each one of us counts—from the high-level executive to the gardener or, as my one friend called me, the family slave. I ask that we keep the belief in ourselves, still look for the good in others, and seriously wish the best for others. We all deserve to be happy, so we keep putting one foot in front of the other as we move through this world. We get only one chance, and that can be taken any minute of the day by our Almighty God.

For those who have supported me by reading my writing: I thank you and appreciate each one of you! Be the light, and let's keep putting those smiles out there. There is too much darkness in our world. My best wishes to each one of you. May you find the light, and even if it is currently just a small sparkle, let it glow and come through your smile. Despite all my darkness, I have seen all the lights and joy thankfully. Life is short; let us make it the best we can with God's and our angels' help. Be your own warrior, and listen to *you*—you have a voice! Mental illness is real. It's OK to be upfront about it. I have hidden it for so many years as it was a weakness, and I had so much guilt. But I know I had and have so much to be thankful for.

Be Your Voice! Use that smile and laughter.